PUSH54, LLC:
FOCUS ON KENYA

TREND LINES WILL OVERCOME HEADLINES

The case for a continued focus on the execution of the Vision 2030 plan

FOCUS ON KENYA:
TREND LINES WILL OVERCOME HEADLINES

PUSH54, LLC

Chicago, USA

July 2014

Push54, LLC is an Africa focused U.S firm providing business and management consulting services, and Africa analytics & research services.

1. Advisory services (Corporate, Institutional, and Government)

- Economic Branding
- Foreign Currency Exchange Risk Management
- International Business Development
- International Treasury System Procurement & Implementation
- Operational Risk
- Organizational Design
- Public Private Partnerships
- Regulatory Risk
- Trade Mission Organization

2. Africa Analytics

- Subscription based service
- Heavy focus on private sector and macro-economic data drivers.
- Our core target audiences are African Diaspora in the U.S, Academia, Financial Institutions, and Corporations with an interest in the African markets, and the African continent itself.

PREFACE

This report is the product of a five month long project by Push54, LLC, working with analysts located in Kenya, Tanzania, and Uganda. We sought to do a deep dive analysis of what Kenya's economy has been up to and what projects are putting Kenya on a growth trajectory that most professionals in the West may not be aware of.

The release of this report, while planned months ahead, comes at a time when Kenya is recovering from the recent tragedy in Nairobi. While the authorities continue getting the city back to normal and mounting a detailed investigation of what happened; Push54, LLC is proceeding with the release of our second report of the Focus on Africa series in part to show solidarity with the victims of the attack, but also to reaffirm the economic story that is Kenya.

As we can see in the markets; Kenya's capital markets and infrastructure projects are still doing well and the country has been able to absorb the shock.

Last summer; I attended a conference in Chicago, IL that brought a Chinese delegation to Chicago to go over the derivatives markets. For those in financial markets, it was right after the MF Global and PFG scandals. One of the Chinese attendees asked a question of his American counterparts on what exactly the delegation was expected to learn from their visit given the advice of oversight and proper operational controls were not being adhered to by MF Global and PFG, two of the most respected brokers in Chicago.

My answer to him was that the United States has overtime built a financial system that was able to absorb shocks and keep functioning. Not just corporate scandals, but sometimes national tragedies. The American financial system is one of the best in history for this exact reason. Its ability and versatility against adversity and being able to digest an event and continuing its role in the American economy.

Kenya and its citizens, including its financial markets has shown that, while smaller in size than the U.S., it was able to absorb the shock of the Mall attack, and continued on its national agenda of economic growth. I was very impressed and so were my colleagues. Kenya's leaders and response teams demonstrated a level of leadership and national togetherness that was exemplary. It validated Kenya's status as one of the great economic and national powers in Africa.

The goals of the Focus report series and Push54's Africa Analytics service is to not only provide our membership with an understanding of what is currently taking place in a particular country or region in Africa, but also provide a forecast of what decisions leaders will have to make and where those decisions may land given the geopolitical economic map and the particular country's demographic trends.

Before concluding, I would like to emphasize that this work is independent and has not been commissioned or sponsored in any way by any business, government, or other institution.

Justin Mahwikizi
Managing Principal of Push54, LLC
July 2014

TABLE OF CONTENTS

INTRODUCTION

Kenya is located at the eastern Coast of Africa.

She is bordered to the South east by; the Indian Ocean Somalia to the East, Ethiopia to the North, South Sudan to the North west Uganda to the west and Tanzania to the South West and South.

Given her strategic geographical location, Kenya is the sea route to a number of Landlocked Countries in the eastern Africa region. These include; D R Congo, Rwanda, Burundi, Uganda, South Sudan and Ethiopia.

Also her geographical location on the equator, that slices Africa into two equal parts, makes Kenya an air transport hub in Africa for it makes air travel to and from the rest of Africa seamless. Kenya also boasts the largest sea Port in east Africa, which also makes her the gateway to large parts of eastern Africa.

Variable	size
Population (2012 est.)	41 million
Pop. Growth rate	3.2 %
GDP (2012 est.)	US$41.84bn
GDP per capita (2011 est.)	$ 1,800
Literacy rate	81%
Doctor/ Patient ratio	5,263
Nurse/patient ratio	1,205
Health facility/pop. ratio	4,996

Kenya is one of the four economic power houses in Africa. The others are Nigeria, South Africa and Egypt. She is the hub of economic activity is eastern Africa, being the largest economy in the East Africa Common market bloc, EACM. The community, which brings together five Countries in east Africa, boasts of a population of 135.4 million and a GDP per capita estimated at US$732. The five Countries are: Tanzania, Uganda, Kenya, Rwanda and Burundi. Both Sudans and Somalia have applied to join in.

Kenya boasts only 30.4 per cent of the bloc's total population. Her GDP, however, estimated at US$ 41.84 billion at the end of last year, forms nearly half of the GDP of EACM, estimated at US$84.7 billion. Kenya's population is estimated at 41.2 million with a per capita GDP estimated at US$1,800.

In the following sections, we look at the current macroeconomic indicators, the leading sectors, and the country's development agenda and how much activity Kenya has been undertaking.

MACROECONOMIC OVERVIEW

At US$41.84 billion, Kenya's economy is the largest in east Africa. The economy has posted consistently robust growth over the 2002-2012 decade. The only blot was the year 2008/09 when the country suffered the ravages of 2007/8 post-election Violence. However, the country has since shrugged off that folly and is back on the growth trajectory. Since 2010, the economy has posted growth rates above 4 per cent. *See Chart 1 below*

Chart 1   *Kenya's Macro-economic indicators 1998-2012*

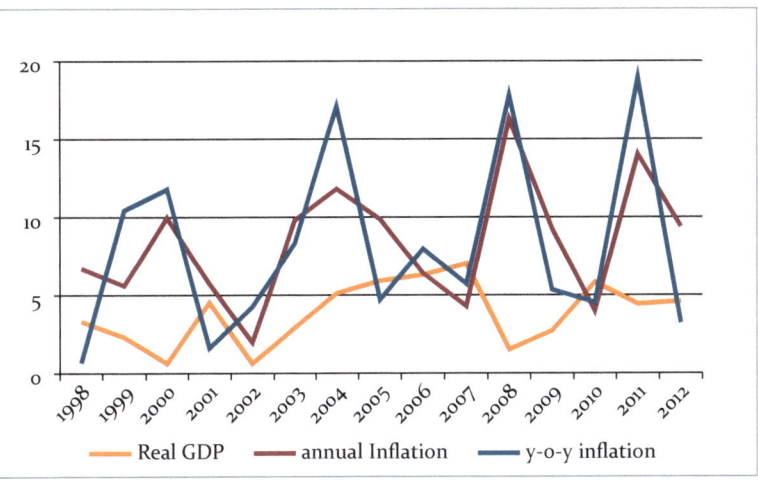

Source: Central Bank of Kenya.

The IMF projects that beginning this year; Kenya will join the ranks of fastest growing economies in Africa. Both the IMF and World Bank project that the Kenyan economy will grow by 5.6-6.0 per cent this year after which it is projected to be growing at above six per cent.

LEADING SECTORS IN KENYAN ECONOMY

The main drivers of the robust growth are Agriculture, Manufacturing, Tourism, and trade in that order. *See Chart 2 below*

Chart 2

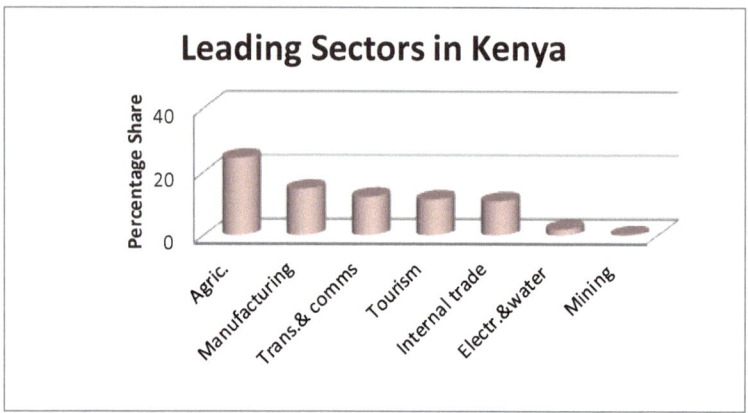

Source: Kenya fact book 2012

AGRICULTURE

Agriculture is the leading sector contributing 21 per cent of the real GDP. It employs a large segment of the labor force. Among the leading cash crops is Tea which last year generated US$1.184 billion in exports earnings. This was a six per cent increase over the US$1.124 billion earned in 2010. Coffee' which was once upon a time the most popular cash crop is sliding down the scale to almost the fourth position after horticulture and tourism in that order.

In Horticulture the leading crop is cut flowers which last year earned US$765 million from exports. Other crops include fruits and vegetables. However this is a growing segment and its importance is likely to rise as large European Chain stores are now contracting local farmers to produce for them. We also see a rise in demand from Asia potentially growing in the near term.

The largest proportion of Agricultural produce is consumed locally. The sector suffers largely from its dependence on rains. This implies that in case of poor rains, agricultural output is low which leads to food insecurity. Food shortages are the main drivers of domestic inflation. During the time of food shortages, inflation skyrockets and dips in times of sufficient food supplies.

To ensure sustainable food supply and eliminate food insecurity, Vision 2030 plans to shift away from rain-fed agriculture to irrigation. There are proposals to create one million hectares of irrigated farms in a bid to eliminate food insecurity. The first phase of this project is already under way where a 146 Km long Dam will be built to hold 5.6 billion Cubic meters of water. Part of this water will be used to irrigate 250,000 hectares of farmland. The project, to be developed on a PPP (Public Private Partnership) basis, will cost an estimated US$1.25 billion. The sector is expected to create another 3 million jobs by 2017, ranging from irrigation workers to agri-business, to agro-processing.

MANUFACTURING

Manufacturing is the second driver of Kenya's economy contributing an estimated 14 per cent of the real GDP. The sector comprises mainly of light manufacturing of consumer goods such as processed foods, personal care items and drinks. There are very little heavy industries although motor vehicle assembling is growing. This is a key recent development we hope to see increase and we hope that more Kenyans gain access to their own cars throughout the whole country in the future. The increase in car ownership would lead to an increase in economic activity allowing an increase in local tourism, and long distance working.

Despite its small size, the sector outperforms all others in export earnings. It is the dominant sector in east Africa and even the COMESA region. Manufactured goods are exported to Uganda, Tanzania and other African markets.

In fact due to exports of manufactured goods, Africa has become Kenya's leading market over shadowing Europe and the USA. Uganda is the leading export destination for Kenya's manufactured exports, followed by Tanzania, both absorb more than US$1 billion which is slightly under 50 per cent of the US$2.9 billion worth of manufactured exports to African markets.

Figure 1 Africa is the top market for Kenya's manufactured goods

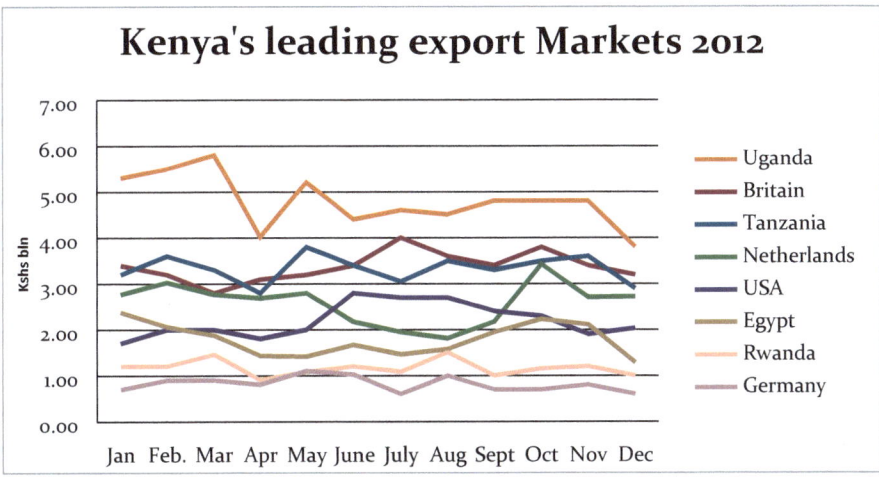

8

This sector operates at 40-50 per cent below capacity due to bottlenecks such as expensive electricity, and small markets. The markets are small in some instances due to lack of physical transport infrastructure. Consequently, the prices of local manufactured goods are high compared to imports of similar goods. The sector is currently operating in vicious cycle of high prices and low demand. The manufacturing sector will be the greatest beneficiary of the on -going investment in infrastructure such as roads, Rails and power generation for they will lower the cost of doing business in addition to opening up new markets. Low prices will in turn lead to higher demand for local goods leading to a further decline in prices and further expansion in demand which will create more jobs in the manufacturing sector.

The sector employed some 275,700 people in 2012 with a job creation rate averaging 1.75 per cent a year. The job creation rate is expected to grow rapidly once the sector's growth picks up.

TOURISM

This is the third largest sector in Forex earnings. In 2011 it earned US$1.15 billion. The sector's main attraction is wildlife and sandy beaches. There has also been a notable growth in business tourism. Kenya is home to the big five - Elephant, Buffalo, Lion, Rhino and Cheetah. These, coupled with sandy beaches attract visitors. Kenya has traditionally relied on the West-Europe and USA for visitors. However, the country is increasingly turning south to expand tourist arrivals from 1.5 million last year to 5 million by 2030.

The south includes such newly rich countries as China, India and South Korea. On a recent trip to China, Kenya's Cabinet Secretary for Foreign Affairs and International made it quite clear that Kenya is working on attracting 3 million Chinese tourists every year. Apart from wildlife and beaches, Vision 2030 also includes the development of Resort cities to diversify and increase the product range. The Five resort cities will include cultural tourism among other products such as movie making. Of the five, three are on the LAPSSET corridor. However, with the discovery of oil in Northern Kenya, these cities viz: Turkana, Isiolo and Lamu are likely to become energy cities in addition to tourism.

It is estimated that 250,000Kenyans work in the tourism sector. Estimates say that every eight tourists create one job. The implication here is: to create more jobs in the sector, Kenya needs to increase the number of visitors in the ratio of 8:1. This implies increasing and diversifying the product range to include cultural, sports and business tourism.

KENYA'S DEVELOPMENT AGENDA

Kenya's development goals are defined in its blue-print for long term development, Vision 2030. The vision aims to "transform Kenya into a newly industrializing, middle-income country providing a high quality of life to all its citizens by 2030 in a clean and secure environment."

To hit the target, the economy must grow at double digits for the next decade and beyond. To grow at double digits requires heavy investment in improved productivity. Although this is an achievable target, there are stumbling blocks and bottlenecks. An "all hands on deck" attitude needs to be adopted by all Kenyans, including the government and their international partners. Distractions that sometimes perk up once in a while present roadblocks to Kenya's economic growth.

With the destination and the travel speed clearly defined, what remains is the road map to the destination. The journey is not smooth as the road is rough full of Potholes, Craters and Gullys that the traveler must deal with on the way. One could decide to use all-terrain vehicles or work to repair or rebuild the roads.

The bottlenecks that could choke Kenya's development agenda are transport and energy infrastructure - roads, railway lines, Seaports, power generation plants and expanded grid; new and expanded airports, Communication networks to enable and support the expansion and transformation of the economy.

Consequently, Kenya has chosen the difficult but in the long term beneficial and sustainable path: rebuilding, expanding and developing new infrastructure facilities. For this reason, the country looks like a huge construction site. This path means heavy financial outlays in infrastructure development. New Projects- from roads to hydro projects, to new geothermal steam wells to wind power farms to expanded new airports and sea ports- the country is awash with massive infrastructure projects. And Greenfield projects in the same areas are in the pipeline or contracts have been awarded and work will begin soon. These projects, according to Vision2030 must be in place by 2030. For lenders, investors and contractors, Kenya's development agenda presents huge business opportunities.

INFRASTRUCTURE DEVELOPMENT

This section is in three segments, namely transport infrastructure, energy infrastructure and ICT. Since the section describes what are by and large work- in- progress projects, it could also be viewed as a description of business opportunities segment.

TRANSPORT INFRASTRUCTURE SECTOR

This section covers the entire range of physical transport infrastructure in the country ranging from roads to seaports, to airports, to railway lines. As stated right from the outset; Transport infrastructure is a major constraint to economic growth in Kenya. This is because all other brick and mortar players need transport infrastructure to reach their markets. Efficient and reliable transport infrastructure lower the cost-of doing business and hence the cost of goods in the domestic economy.

Kenya is well situated as a transport hub. It is traversed by three major transport corridors namely the Great North road (GNR) from Cape town in South Africa to Cairo in Egypt; the trans Africa Highway from Mombasa in Kenya to Lagos in Nigeria.

The Great North Road is among the three roads that link Kenya to Tanzania, her neighbor to the South. This road has been widened and improved between Arusha in Tanzania and the Mombasa Road Junction in Athi River, Kenya.

There is also a branch road off Northern Corridor highway linking Voi in Kenya and Moshi in Tanzania. This is under-construction. It is one of those roads that Kenya and Tanzania undertook jointly. The other was the Arusha –Athi River section of the GNR. There is also a road from Mombasa Port to Dar-Es-Salaam, Tanzania's commercial capital through Tanga, a port city in Tanzania.In fact Kenya is over-connected with Tanzania, by road and air. Kenya airways, the dominant airline in east Africa, in fact parks some of her Aircraft at Dar-Es-salaam International Airport.

Apart from Trans Africa highway and the GNR, Kenya is also the origin of the proposed equator land bridge, a Railway line from Lamu Port in Kenya on the Indian Ocean coast, to Douala in Cameroon on the Atlantic Ocean coast. The "bridge" once complete will cut the transit period for imports to, and export from Africa by three weeks. However that project is still on the drawing board. It should be noted though that, the Kenyan section of equator- Bridge also doubles as the Lamu Port, South Sudan Ethiopia Transport Corridor.

Of these corridors, the most active is the Northern transport Corridor. This is part of the Trans Africa highway. The Northern Corridor is a 3500Km long stretching from the Mombasa Port in Kenya, to Bujumbura in Burundi through Uganda and Rwanda. It will be extended to South Sudan through Eldoret, Kenya. It comprises of a sea Port, a road, a Railway line and an oil Pipeline. It is therefore the gateway to the sea for South Sudan, Uganda, Burundi, Rwanda and eastern D R Congo

MOMBASSA PORT

At the foot of the Corridor is the Mombasa Port in Kenya. This is the largest Port in east Africa which handles exports and imports for five countries: Kenya, South Sudan, Uganda, Rwanda, Burundi and eastern D R Congo.

The Port has come under intense pressure owing to robust economic growth in its hinterland and the growth of vessel sizes. It was designed to handle only about 5 million tons of Cargo a year but increased demand has stretched its capacity to bursting point. It now handles four-times its design capacity. For instance, last year, the Port handled close to 20 million tons. Its container terminal, which was designed to handle 250,000TEUs, handled 900,000 TEUs last year. This four-fold growth in demand amidst a static Port led to massive inefficiencies and the related high cost of doing business in the region.

Figure 2. Mombasa Port

The Port is now undergoing a US$350 million expansion programme to transform it into a Mega Port. The first phase of the project, which involved drenching and widening of the Port, is complete enabling it to berth three Post-panamax vessels simultaneously.

That has made a bad situation worse as the Port can now off-load large quantities of Cargo on a limited space. However, just last month, the Port commissioned berth No 19 with a capacity of 200,000TEUs. This berth has increased the container handling capacity to 450,000 TEUs, a welcome relief considering that previously, the Port could handle 900,000TEUs in container terminal designed for 250,000TEUs. However, the on-going construction of the second Container terminal will increase the Port's capacity to 2.1 million TEUs. The second Terminal will be completed in two years' time by the end of 2015.

Expansion of the Sea capacity has created a huge capacity problem on the land. The Mombasa city now suffers chronic traffic jams due to heavy traffic from the Port. There are an estimated 20,000 long haul trucks calling at the Port a year to ferry cargo to as far as

Figure 3: Prototype of Dogo Kundu by-pass

Burundi. Simple averaging shows that there are 55 long-haul trucks on the road from the Port to Nairobi highway every day.

This is in addition to short haul trucks which run into hundreds. That is why there is a road project planned to by-pass the city. The Mombasa Southern by-pass popularly known as Dogo Kundu will link the port to the Trans-Africa highway at Miritini, 19 Km away from the City. The project will be funded by JICA (Japan International Cooperation Agency).

THE MOMBASSA PORT – KIGALI SG RAILWAY LINE

To make the port more efficient, Kenya, Uganda, Rwanda and Burundi- all members of the northern corridor- have agreed to build a 3500Km long high speed Railway line from Mombasa to Kigali in Rwanda and onto Bujumbura, Burundi.

The Project was initially designed to begin from Mombasa and terminate in Kigali Rwanda at a cost of US$13.5 billion to build and equip. However, the governments concerned agreed to extend it to Burundi and South Sudan. However, each country will finance its section of the new railway line.

Kenya has already sourced US$2.75 billion from China to build her section of the Railway line. The line will cost US$2.4 billion and the rest will purchase rolling stock. Construction of the Kenyan side of the Railway line will commence in November 2013. It shall be completed in 2017. On Completion the Railway line will cut the time it takes to ship freight from Mombasa to Nairobi from 10 hour to 4 hours. Cargo will be able to move

Kenya-Uganda Railway: To remain under concession

From Mombasa to Kigali in just two days. Currently it takes up to 10 days to travel this stretch.

This railway line will be the second line after the 100 year-old narrow gauge Kenya-Uganda railway. The Railway line has been concessioned to Rift Valley railways for 25 years.

Although the concession has not been successful, the operator is also improving on its rolling stock in a bid to stake a claim on the massive business on in the offing.

THE LAMU PORT – SOUTH SUDAN – ETHIOPIA CORRIDOR

The US$25.5billion Lamu Port - South Sudan- Ethiopia Transport Corridor (LAPSSET), is the biggest business venture ever to be undertaken in east Africa and probably beyond. It will link Kenya to Ethiopia and South Sudan.

LAPSSET, comprises of; 1,710 KM of standard Gauge railway line, 880 KM of a standard highway, 1260 KM of crude oil pipeline, 980KM of white oils pipeline, a 120,000 bpd refinery, a 32 berths sea port, three resort cities and two international Airports.

The resort cities are meant to diversify product offering and increase tourism in the arid but high potential lands. The cities are Lamu, Isiolo and Turkana resort cities. However, with the discovery of oil in Turkana County, the cities, which will cost US$220 million apiece, could become energy cities with Tourism as a side-show. Construction of the US$12 million Isiolo international airport -which is one of the two airports planned - is complete. Lamu Airport is yet to begin as it is awaiting the completion of the first three of the 32 berth Sea Port. Construction of the three berths which will enable ferrying of building materials inland has already began.

Lamu Port Berth Design Layout
Bird's-eye View of First Three Berths of Lamu Port

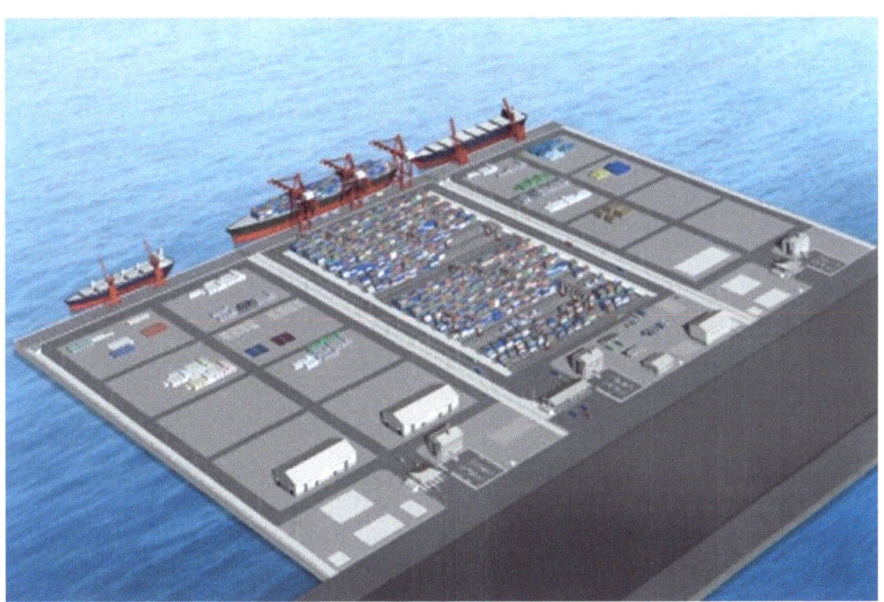

Apart from the Airports, LAPSSET also includes the construction of a 2000KM High speed railway line from Lamu to juba in South Sudan at a cost of US$8 billion. The line is a section of the proposed Equatorial Land Bridge linking the Port of Lamu on the Indian Ocean to the East to the Port of Doula in Cameroon on the Atlantic Ocean to the West. Such a link, it is envisaged, will cut freight travel time by at least two to three weeks and increase shipping lines' turn-around times and hence their revenue.

LAPSSET initially seemed like a pipedream to pessimists. However, the discovery of commercially viable oil deposits in Northern Kenya has made the project necessary and viable. This is because the corridor will transport crude oil from South Sudan, Kenya and Uganda. It will also transport white oils to Ethiopia. At the time of the study, long before oil was discovered in Uganda and Kenya, the project's IRR was pegged at 14 per cent but with changed fortunes, IRR is slightly higher.

THE JKIA GREENFIELD PROJECT

In addition to the construction of an International airport in Isiolo, contracts have also been awarded for the construction of Greenfield terminal at Nairobi's Jomo Kenyatta International airport, JKIA. The terminal, to be built on a Design-build Finance and Operate (DBFO) basis, will expand JKIA's capacity by 12 million passengers to more than 20 million passengers a year. It will have a parking capacity, including "remote parking" for 60 aircraft, raising the airport's parking slots to over a hundred aircraft.

The Greenfield terminal will have a floor area of 172, 000 sq. m. It will be the premier hub terminal in Africa equipped for efficient connectivity for transiting passengers.

It will have 50 international and 10 domestic check-in positions; 32 contact and 8 remote gates; an apron with 45 stands and linking taxiways and a Railway terminal.

Fig.4 Prototype of Unit 4 at Terminal one, JKIA

The terminal complements a five- year development plan that began in 2007 to expand the capacity of the airport from 2.5 million people a year to 6 million to date. The previous expansion plan which incorporates the construction of unit 4 of terminal one increased the size by creating a parking for 37 aircraft up from 20 previously. This phase cost a whopping US$200 million.

The new terminal, once complete will make Jomo Kenyatta International Airport, JKIA, the aviation hub of East and central Africa.

Reports indicate that the government is looking for land to develop a second runway at JKIA. The idea is to exploit and entrench Nairobi's geographical advantage, which makes it the natural aviation hub of Africa. Already, JKIA is the busiest cargo hub in Africa, handling some 30 Million tons of cargo a year. The cargo is mainly Horticulture and floriculture products from Kenya and the East Africa region.

 The transport and communications sector in Kenya is the fastest growing in Kenya posting an average job creation rate of 4.5 per year. It employed 157,400 people in 2012. The sector is expected to create more jobs following its capacity expansion.

THE ENERGY INFRASTRUCTURE SECTOR

In chart2, we demonstrated the leading sectors of the economy and then slipped in Electricity and water almost at the bottom end. The Purpose was to demonstrate the potential bottlenecks. Electric energy, like transport infrastructure is a major bottleneck to Kenya's development agenda. The major source of electricity generation is hydro which is prone to vagaries of weather. The supply is thus unreliable. To cushion drought related unreliability, the country resorts to expensive thermal (diesel powered) electricity which is expensive.

During droughts, the cost of living shoots up as the cost of power rises. In such times, the cost of fossil fuels used to generate power forms between 35 and 70 per cent of every dollar spend on power. This cost is passed on to the consumers of industrial goods.

Hydro for now forms the bulk of electricity generated in the country (766.88MW) which forms 65 per cent KenGen's installed capacity. KenGen is the power generating utility. Kenya's generating capacity of 1400MW serves only 14 per cent of the Population. And the power is expensive.

VISION **2030** ENERGY TARGETS

The country plans to increase its power generating capacity by 17,000MW by the year 2030 when it will transit to an emerging economy status. The capacity currently is less than 1,500 MW hence the mad rush to hit targets in just 17 years. The budget for this exercise is US$42.5 billion or US$2.5 billion a year, which makes electricity generation a hot investment in the country.

Power source	Potential (MW)	Exploited (MW)	Outstanding(MW)
Hydro	1600	818	782
Geothermal	7000	992.5*	6007.5
Wind	3000	656.8*	2343.2
Solar	N/A	N/A	N/A

Fig.4   Power generation sources in Kenya and their potential

In the Medium term, the country has investments in place that will double the power supply to more than 3000MW by 2016. Of these, KenGen, the leading power generator in the country will produce 2,364MW. The Geothermal Development Corporation (GDC) will produce another 400MW of geothermal. A private company, Lake Turkana Wind power Ltd, is also expected to generate another 300MW of wind power into the nation grid. At this point, owing to a dominance of clean energy sources, the cost of power is expected to shrink to US$0.08 per KWh from the current US$0.14 which sometimes rises to 20 US cents. Eventually the cost is expected to shrink to $0.06 per KWh before 2030.

Although, electricity generation is liberalized, there are two Major electricity generators in Kenya. These are the KenGen and GDC. Both are State Owned Enterprises (SOEs). However, KenGen is partially privatized and is therefore listed at the Nairobi Securities Exchange. KenGen generates power from all sources including Hydro, Thermal, Geothermal, Wind power and Coal.

Being the oldest power generation firm-and the best capitalized-, it is expected to generate 10,000MW of the 17,000MW needed in 2030.

The other Public owned generator is Geothermal Development Corporation, GDC. A recent creation, GDC specializes in generating geothermal power. It is currently developing 400MW-almost 26 per cent of the current capacity- of geothermal power from its Menengai fields that will come on grid in 2016. The firm hopes to generate a further 3000MW of by 2020 from the same fields rising to 5500MW in 2031.

The private sector has found it very difficult to enter into electricity generation due to the high capital requirement. For instance, the US$750 million Lake Turkana wind power project, which is the largest wind power project in Africa, has been trying to raise debt finance for nearly Seven years. The project began to look viable when Africa Development Bank lend it US$250 million early this year. Reports have it that more investors have trooped in and are negotiating senior debt arrangements with AfDB, the lead arranger.

However, given the level of demand and the investment needed, the public sector will play a huge part in electricity generation into the future.

Figure 4 above shows the available sources of electricity generation in the country and how much of it is exploited. From the table only Hydro is in a large part exploited. The little that remains will come from water harvesting by increasing the height of the existing hydro dam. Aside from hydro, other sources of electricity are under-exploited. The asterisk show just what is planned for exploitation in the next three to five years. For example only about 62MW of wind are in Use out of the potential 3000MW. Geothermal potential is 7000MW but only about 250MW is now operational. The rest will come on stream in the course of the next three years.

Although the space for solar is marked N/A, solar energy is ubiquitous in Kenya. However, it is not easy to put tag on the quantity available for now, Kenya being a country on the equator. Unlike other sources, solar can be customized for consumer need, small panels for small consumers and bigger panels for big consumers. It is a high potential resource and like wind, there is no drilling risk.

The country will have to employ a mix of financial models ranging from good old PPA-power Purchase Agreements; to PPP; to joint ventures, to imports, borrowing from DFIs and the local and international Capital markets.

The private sector which is averse to the drilling risk is not averse to the generation risk. Therefore we expect to see an increase in Private-Public partnerships in the energy sector. The private sector could sign long-term PPA with the power distribution company, and then use such contracts to borrow from the market.

Already the government business model is designed to draw in the private sector. GDC for instance will undertake the drilling risk where it will drill steam wells, cap them and then lease them to the private sector to build generation plants. This will release funds and personnel to GDC to develop further wells while the private sector manages the daily generation and maintenance functions.

Ken Gen is the largest power generator in the country, partially privatized. It therefore exercise some degree of autonomy is its investment plans. It can borrow through capital market instruments such as infrastructure bonds. So far it has US$300 million worth of long-term infrastructure bonds in the market. It is also crafting the first asset backed Bond in the market. The firm hopes to borrow at least US$350-400 million using this instrument. Asset backed bonds require the creation of an SPV, to whom the assets are transferred. The SPV will then borrow from the market and transfer the money to KenGen. It will then sale the power generated and use the funds to service the bond. This model reduced KenGen's debt burden, enabling it to raise funds to develop further generating capacity. Power generation is a high return investment avenue in Kenya.

This sector together with water employed 174,600 people in 2012. According to the Kenya factbook2012, employment in this sector grows, on average, at 2.2 per cent a year. This is expected to rise as more generation capacity comes on stream.

TELECOMMINUCATIONS AND ICT INFRASTRUCTURE

According to the communications Commission of Kenya, mobile tele-density as at the end of March, 2013 was 75.6 per cent. That is, of Kenya's population estimated at 40 million, 29.8 million are mobile phone subscribers and almost 15 million internet subscribers. This high rate of penetration was driven by low cost of making a call at US$0.04 per minute. The low cost was in turn enabled by low rates of connectivity due to availability of low cost undersea fiber optic links.

At the moment Kenya has four undersea cables including EASSy, TEAMS, SEACOM, and LION-2, which hold more than 2.8 terabytes of bandwidth. A fifth one is said to be in the pipeline. This will increase Kenya's capacity to 15 terabytes. At home the country is ringed by an estimated 30,000Km of terrestrial cables and is still counting. The mobile telecommunications sector has created an estimated 300,000 jobs in the informal sector.

Such ease of communication capacity has spawned the growth of ICT industry in Kenya which led to the conception and birth of a techno city.

Konza Techno City is a US$7 billion project located just 60Km South West of Nairobi and 50Km from JKIA. Set on a 2000 hectare piece of land, Konza is arguably the first city of its kind in Africa. It will comprise of a Central Business District, and BPO Park, a university, other schools; and a financial district. It will also host shopping malls, hospitals and residential estates.

Dubbed the Silicon savannah, Konza Techno city is designed to enable Kenya to compete neck to neck with global giants in BPO, KPO and ITOs including India, China, and The Philippines. On the African continent, Kenya will compete with South Africa and Egypt. Being the first city of its kind in the East Africa common Market bloc, Konza is likely to be the regional technology hub. It is fronted by three of the four Marine cables that have already landed in Kenya.

The ICT Park is allocated 1.4 million M^2 of land reflecting the importance the government attaches to technology development. It will be flanked by a Science Park 226,000M^2. The Central Business District which shall comprise of mixed use commercial blocs including Shopping malls and Restaurants is allocated 669,000M^2 of land.

The city is expected to contain 37,000 homes for its 300,000 citizens. Zoned in four clusters ranging from very high density to low density dwellings the residential zone's area is 3.6 million M^2.

The city's ground breaking, ceremony was held in January 2013 and construction has begun. First off the block is work on the infrastructure, roads and water and waste water disposal systems. Already; a US$200 million multipurpose water dam funded by the Kenya government is under construction and is expected to be complete by October 2013. The dam will pump one million liters of water to the city a day.

Figure 5 A prototype of Konza Techno City

Several contractors are already in place. Among these is the Master Planner, HR & A advisors of New York. A Chinese Construction Company, Shanghai Corporation for Foreign Economic & Technological Cooperation (SFECO) is constructing roads and other social infrastructure. A Swedish firm has bagged the tender to develop the science park and market it among investors.

Also in the queue for various segments of the project, are other experienced developers such as Egypt's Smart Villages and the Korea Business Centre. The intense interest in the project is not surprising as returns on investment are mouth-watering. For instance, return on leasing ranges between 12 and 15 per cent while capital gains rate is estimated at 20 per cent. The city will create an estimated 200,000 ICT related jobs.

THE BUSINESS PROCESS OUTSOURCING (BPO) INDUSTRY

Of all the potential segments in the outsourcing sector, that is BPO, KPO and ITOs only BPOs are known in Kenya. By 2012, the sector had created 7,500 jobs which are expected to rise to 20,000 jobs next year. However the sector has been hampered by the slow growth of demand. In fact, those that are operating are sourcing contracts from within the region. Foreign contracts are still not forthcoming. This is mainly due to poor marketing of Kenya as a BPO destination.

The country boasts of a well-educated, accent-neutral English speaking relatively low-cost labor force. The country also boasts of five marine cable networks with a total capacity of 5.3 terabytes which is expected to rise to 15 terabytes once the fifth cable lands.

Push54, LLC is a big proponent for Kenya being considered as a strong alternative BPO destination.

REAL ESTATE DEVELOPMENT

Two developments in the recent past have made the acute shortage of houses prominent. Of course Kenya has always suffered a shortage of decent housing. In fact demand outstrips supply by far. Annual demand for houses is 150,000 units while only35, 000 units are built every year. This leaves a yawning gap of 115,000 units. Due to this gap, the units developed only meet the latent demand. This is not to be considered as a defect but rather as an opportunity.

Robust economic growth of the last decade has pushed the cost of housing way beyond the reach of many in the growing middle class. New and reliable roads have pushed the middle class into satellite cities but still the cost of housing keeps rising.

 Economic theory dictates that where there is shortage, prices rise and when demand meets supply, prices stabilize and even decline.

Economic prosperity coupled with the promulgation of the new constitution has only pushed up demand for housing while supply is relatively static. The constitution has created 47 new county governments thus spreading demand for quality houses to the counties.

High costs of anything, economic theory dictates, are a pointer to opportunities to meet the demand. Therefore investors, both domestic and foreign, should investigate further the opportunities that Kenya may be presenting. The market is liberalized and therefore open to all investors.

THE MINING SECTOR

The mining sector is a relatively new entrant in Kenya's economic scene. In fact, it does not even feature in Vision 2030, Kenya's long- term development blue-print. However, a string of discoveries especially of Oil Coal has changed the picture. Mining must now be incorporated into Kenya's development plan. An estimated 400 million tons of coal have been discovered in Mui Basin in Mwingi Country in eastern Kenya.

The discovery of commercially viable crude oil deposits in Turkana County recently has catapulted mining onto the front bench. It is not clear how much oil lies in Kenya's territory but estimates have been rising every few months. The latest such estimate has placed the available quantity at more than 360 million barrels. Other estimates suggest that Kenya could be sitting on at least 10 billion barrels of crude - enough to feed the US for 18 months. At the current consumption levels in Kenya, the estimates say, this quantity could last Kenya for 300 years. The discovery of Crude oil has spawned a stampede among oil Majors and oil Juniors for exploratory licenses for LNG and crude oil. Other findings include Titanium, which is expected to earn Kenya US$250 million a year for the next 13 years. Reports of findings of other minerals deposits have surfaced but are yet to be confirmed by competent authorities. The government has even warned oil prospectors against announcing finds without first consulting with it.

CONCLUSION AND RECOMMENDATION

Kenya is on track to achieving vision 2030 goals. There are large investments in areas of physical infrastructure that would improve productivity in the private sector. Efficient production and distribution means lead to lower prices. In fact the government has set low essential goods prices as a major plank of its economic policy. Low prices increase demand for goods and therefore consumption leading to further growth. The country has already missed the target of 12 per cent growth from 2012 onwards. However, this is not a far off dream. It is achievable.

But the investment outlay required is very high. Already gross national debt has hit 52 per cent of the GDP or US$21.8 billion. Much of the funds are borrowed for development of physical infrastructure given the low uptake by the private sector of opportunities available.

The low uptake is understandable. Even the private sector would have to seek debt finance to fund some of the physical infrastructure projects for they need huge financial outlay. The private sector does not have the stomach for the high risk associated with the initial sunk capital in either road construction or drilling a steam well.

This means that the Kenya government has to continue taking the high sunk capital risk in order to hasten development of infrastructure to support rapid economic growth.

Kenya must identify some "heavy traffic" infrastructure projects such as roads, steam wells, sea ports, railway lines and airports, to transfer to the private sector through the PPP arrangement. This will divest the government of the operation and maintenance risk to the private sector and further generate finances for the government through the royalties and taxes levied on the operators. This way, the country will generate funds from the projects to service the debts used to develop them

Where the Private sector is ready to take all risks, such as in oil drilling and crude oil transportation, the government should license such operators and only charge royalties and taxes.

What most miss, however, and what stands to be the biggest opportunity for Kenyans, regional Africans and other entrepreneurs are the markets these projects are bound to create and/or facilitate. Roads and Railways present opportunities for retail lodgments, and restaurants that service travelers. From the most basic needs of customers in different towns to the ability to relay commodity price fluctuations across towns and countries that was not possible before will bring Africans closer. Better data will allow Bankers to better assess Farming lending risk.

African Capital markets will deepen. The bottom line is that all these trends in Kenya that show the intense work the country has been undertaking with collaboration of international partners, African and otherwise, lead one to see the possibility that this foundation will provide citizens and immigrants alike.

When Kenya achieves most of these projects; the early investors and participants will have put themselves in a position to enjoy the rewards for decades. It is for this reason, we at Push54 recommend for the region to stay the course and keep executing on the plan. There will be noise and tragedies along the way. Those will be dealt by authorities and Kenyans will come together in those moments of national tragedies. When the vision is achieved; Kenya will have done the serious work that allows East Africa to be one of the most followed economic stories of this century.

CONTACTS

PUSH54, LLC

Justin Mahwikizi
Managing Principal
Justin.mahwikizi@push54.com

General inquiries
Push54, LLC
One South Dearborn
Suite 2100
Chicago, IL 60603
(800) 267-7167
info@push54.com

 **In line with Push54, LLC's commitment to minimize its impact on the environment, this document has been printed on paper with a high recycled content.**

www.push54.com

www.ingramcontent.com/pod-product-compliance
Lightning Source LLC
Chambersburg PA
CBHW040916180526
45159CB00010BA/3088